MW00891049

Tales from the Men of the Sweetheart Gang

Compiled by
Rev. Dorothy Scott Boulware
Author of *Make yourself at home in God's love*

Tales from the Men of the Sweetheart Gang

For information on this and other publications,
Visit WalkingWorthyNow.com

Dedication

To the fathers. All the fathers. Especially the fathers of these "Daddy's Girls" who just couldn't pass up an opportunity to brag about their fathers. One was a master builder. One was a doctor. Another was a stalwart man of prayer. More than one presented as closet philosophers, community leaders, men of principle. Men who "fathered" more than their own children in the neighborhood.

All of them left lasting impressions, indelible love prints in the hearts of these daughters who delight in telling their stories. They are the husbands, lovers and friends – the Men of the Sweetheart Gang.

And in case this is your first "Sweetheart" encounter, you'll want to know the origin of the name.

The women in my childhood came in all shapes and sizes. They were hard and harsh. They were soft and squishy. They were affectionate and loving. They were faithful and fearless. They were peaceful and forgiving. They always had candy in their purses and usually smelled like peppermint. But the thing I loved best is that they called me "Sweetheart." Now something in my "little girl" mind thought that at some point in life, a button was pushed inside them and immediately and spontaneously, little old ladies began to call everyone Sweetheart. I thought it was the most wonderful thing. I'd never had a nickname, a thing I'd always considered a sign of love. So it tickled my fancy to hear these little ladies call me Sweetheart. Ladies at church. Ladies in the neighborhood; the ones I ran errands for and whose front steps I scrubbed. I didn't mind at all because they called me Sweetheart. I couldn't wait to become one of them and become all sweet and squishy and call everybody Sweetheart. I was sure it was one of those progressive steps to becoming an angel in heaven. Little did I know it was all a ruse. They weren't that progressively sweet and squishy. And do you know how I found out? I got old. I was already squishy. And I began to call people Sweetheart because I couldn't remember their names. What a raw deal! My desired elevation was simply a coverup for an elusive memory.

Featured fathers are Eddie Radden Jr.,

James Edward Byrd Jr., Oscar Lee
Boulware, Dr. Jether M. Jones Jr., Joseph
Levi Blackwell, Eddie Owens Crest,
David Michael Ginyard and Richard
McGuire Diggs.

Table of Contents

Chapters:

Dancing with Daddy

By Bishop Robbin Blackwell, daughter of Joseph Levi Blackwell

Several months ago, I was talking to someone about the struggle of maintaining a rhythm in our relationship with the Lord. The question I proposed was "when you were growing up as a little girl did you ever dance with your father … with your feet on top of his? Who was leading…keeping the rhythm? She immediately grasped the image. And so do I. I am a Daddy's girl and as I enter into this mature season of my life I am realizing how much of my rhythm of life springs from "Dancing with Daddy."

My daddy, Joseph Levi Blackwell, was one of seven children born in the Northern Neck of Virginia around 1912. He was next to the youngest with a younger sister who was his heart. Daddy was a paradox. On the one hand he was a man with a strong work ethic with a no-nonsense attitude about the basics of life. On the other hand, he was what some of the elders would call a "rascal." He loved a good time, laughter and one could never quite know whether or not the twinkle in his eye was a sign of something mischievous.

Case in point, when Joe Blackwell was probably in his late seventies, he decided that he was 80 years old and wanted to celebrate. I'm dancing with Daddy, so I throw an 80th birthday party for him at my home. His friends from church, community and some family members all came bearing $80 gifts! It was a great party and he almost got away with it. But one of the honored guests was his older cousin, Lottie. Cousin Lottie, leaning on her cane in conversation says "You know Joe, you are not eighty; I was there and I remember when you were born. But this is a nice party! Dancing with Daddy the rascal.

 I was an adopted child. I came to Joe and Pearl as a small infant, a few months old. Most people considered my mother the primary parent. I was raised by "her village" (her 11 brothers and sisters). Daddy was not visibly involved in every aspect of my life. Today we would say, he was not a helicopter parent. But he established a relationship of trust with me in his own way. He operated in what I call a Deuteronomy 11 parenting style. (Teach your children when you are sitting in your house, or walking the streets, when you get up, when you lay down...). Daddy made no great fanfare about being a father, but he was ALWAYS talking.

One of my earliest memories of Daddy is as a toddler. He worked as an electrical worker on the midnight shift. When he came home in the morning he would clean up, give my mother the car to go to work and walk me to daycare a few blocks away. When I got older, he walked me to elementary school, again a few blocks away, talking the entire time. Eventually, we bargained as to how far he could walk me and then watch me the rest of the way...Daddy's girl but growing up. We both adapted.

I am coming to realize that my ministry style and mentoring / coaching methodology springs from dancing with Daddy … always teaching and imparting along the way.

Daddy had an 8th grade education. He was big on education as it concerned me in a no-nonsense manner. Once he told me what he expected, there was no need to revisit the matter. He was diligent in providing a good education. One of the lessons learned dancing with Daddy is that "book learning" as he called it is good, but not the paramount thing. His desire for me was that I would just use common sense. In those times when I had clearly done something unwise, his line was, "I have spent over $100,000 on your education and you still don't have any common sense." Thus I inherited what my circle of close friends have called LTI, a low tolerance for ignorance.

Daddy often told me that he would come and get me out of anything except if I ran out of gas, because he considered it stupid. It has only happened to me once and I felt like a moron. The lesson imparted is that you plan for everything and plan around whatever circumstances you find yourself in, don't just go rushing along in life. I continue to struggle with that dance step, but not because it was not taught.

The other dance step I struggle with is the "pile," which was Daddy's lesson in economics and finances. The pile was something you consistently and regularly added to and for the most part never took away from. His point was that you only took from the pile in extreme emergencies and as a last resort, because once you took from the pile it was a near impossibility to put it back. This is basically savings 101. The principle served him well throughout his life.

Daddy was raised in the Zion Baptist Church in Lottsburg, Virginia. In his day it was a small clapboard country church with wooden floors, sitting on the hill. I believe Daddy knew Jesus back then but his transforming encounter with the Savior happened on the "other side." You see I lost Daddy twice in my lifetime before he was promoted to Glory.

On a hot summer day when I was a teenager, we were on a staycation while my mother was on vacation in Hawaii. After having a few beers, Daddy decided to do some painting on our back porch and while climbing the ladder, he hit his head. He wouldn't see about it until my mother returned a couple days later. To make a long story short, he underwent brain surgery for the clot that had formed on his brain. He literally died on the table. He was able to describe what he saw before they resuscitated him. After that he talked about his Savior differently than he had before. His focus in life was somehow different than it had been before. He did things with an urgent purpose. He witnessed the miracle to anyone who would listen to him. He traded the bottle for the Bible. He formed different relationships than he had before. His relationship with the church was different than it was before. He did ministry with our pastor and the other deacons. The only thing that remained constant and consistent is that Daddy was still always talking.

Much to my chagrin, Daddy had a source for his talking now with which you couldn't argue. I often tell people that I learned scripture as a teenager because it was Daddy's rod and staff. For whatever trouble I managed to get into, there was a scripture. So much so that he would begin the scripture and I would finish it. Those times when I had really been a terror it was Amos 4:12. He would say "Prepare," and I would say "…to meet my God"! But on this side of life Daddy had the scriptures with him most of the time. His time at home after his retirement consisted of dedicated time in that big black KJV bible that he held on his lap. I gradually learned a different kind of dance with Daddy. This was the dance of impartation. I received an impartation of the value of the word of God in life and living. He was seized by the affection of the Father, and when the time was right in my life, I already knew how such a conversion looked. I love the word of God largely because it was imparted to me in real time and not just as the script of an old ancient text. It was from Joe Blackwell that I learned all I have is what He (the Lawd) said. Whether it was the melody of the word of God or sometimes the cacophony of the word of God, our dance repertoire was ever expanding.

Joseph Blackwell was a man of balance. I prefer to say that he had rhythm. He taught me there is an art to staying in sync with the music of your soul. Growing up in a traditional Baptist setting, his exposure to women in ministry was minimal. But he always expressed his support and constantly encouraged me in ministry. Upon embarking on my first full-time ministry assignment he gave me a word of counsel that has been a guiding force throughout the years. He said "Don't allow ministry to mess up your relationship with the Lord." On more than one occasion after watching me rip and run in ministry assignments, he would admonish me to come away for a while. Daddy understood the rhythm of work and rest. He understood that working in the traditional church is anti-rhythm; that working for the Lord can shut you off or distract you. He also understood the time, space and attention it takes to sustain an intimate relationship with the Lord. In dancing with Daddy I learned to lean in and let him lead. Consequently, it is not difficult most of the time to lean in and allow the Holy Spirit to lead.

Daddy became an ordained deacon. He was also a worshipper. It was nothing to see Deacon Joe at the front of the church clapping his hands and weeping. Yes Daddy was a crying man. Daddy often referred to the scripture "They that sow in tears shall reap in joy. He that goeth forth and weepeth bearing precious seed, shall doubtless come again with rejoicing bringing his sheaves with him" (Psalm 126:5-6) I am more of a reserved person in public but the lesson I learned from a worshipping, crying father was the power of tears in worship and prayer.

Country born and raised, Joseph Blackwell was a gardener and a giver. Tomatoes, cucumbers and other vegetables were planted in his tiny back yard. The neighbors reaped the benefit of the harvest. Lesson learned is the community benefits from your harvest. Well Daddy's community paid for their vegetables by lending an ear to Mr. Blackwell as he talked, testified of the goodness of the Lord and told various and sundry stories. After a passage of time he would hand them a bag of his homegrown vegetables. Daddy loved to talk. All he needed was a warm body with ears attached to be in the same room.

One of the last lessons I learned and counsel I received from Daddy was to "know what season you are in and govern yourself accordingly." Remember the lesson imparted about planning for everything and planning around whatever circumstances in which you find yourself? Well when he knew he was firmly entrenched in his winter season he began to make provisions for living in the winter. Still in his right mind but in the winter he decided to stop driving on his own. He decided to curtail his ministry trips with the funeral brigade bringing comfort to the bereaved. He only went when he really felt like it. He gave up his car saying he could catch the bus to the bank because he banked across from the courthouse and there would always be guards present. He informed me that I was to drive him if he needed to go somewhere else. He walked everywhere else in the community he needed to go. He knew what season he was in and governed himself accordingly.

The second time I lost Daddy before his promotion to Glory happened not too many months after his winter season decision. On a summer day, he walked to a neighborhood store about four blocks away. On his way home, he became the victim of a hit and run. Witnesses and the police say he was knocked about 60 feet into the air. The woman driving the car kept going. Witnesses chased the car and got the license tag number. Awaking in Shock Trauma a few days later, the talker's voice had changed again. This time there were fewer words. This time it was not the heaven of our understanding that became his world, but a sort of parallel universe. The medical profession called it trauma induced dementia or something like that. To save us both the frustration, I entered his world and stopped trying to bring him back to ours.

I never really saw the Daddy I had known again. His talking gradually slowed until it stopped. No more stories, no more testimonies, no more jokes, no words of wise counsel. The music stopped. There was loud silence. There was sacred stillness on the dance floor. I have learned to make peace with stillness and silence. That was Daddy's last gift to me, his last lesson. The voice of God is so clear and distinct in stillness and silence.

After rehab, home and an assisted living stint, Daddy went into the hospital for surgery. After a few weeks in the hospital we transferred him to a nursing home around midnight one night. He transitioned less than 12 hours later, smiling at the nurse who was bringing him lunch.

I am grateful for the lessons I learned on the dance floor with Daddy. He was a good teacher. Now I can dance in my worship. I can dance as the Lord rejoices over me with singing. I can only imagine his DANCING IN GLORY!

'Tis Better Further On'

By Rev. Dr. Bertha Borum, daughter of Hasel Q. Borum

Every woman who was blessed to have her father in her life to nurture and to love her into womanhood comes to understand that this man named "Daddy" is actually her first love. It is he who will be the standard against which every other man in her life will be measured.

So it was with me and my Dad – Hasel Q. Borum – born January 1, 1910 in Gloucester, Va. He was the eldest of three children who were sadly orphaned by the time he was seven years old. His paternal grandmother Bertha Ann took them in and raised them. It is she for whom I am named.

She had long since gone on to glory before I was born, but Daddy talked about her so much that I felt I had grown up with her too. She was very poor – having very little but a small dirt patch of a farm with a few cows and chickens way back up in the woods and little or no education. What she had in abundance apparently was strong faith, a tremendous prayer life, and great love for her little orphaned grandchildren.

These circumstances helped shape Daddy into the man I knew. He managed to get an eighth grade education before having to quit school and find whatever work he could to earn something to help take care of the family.

In the late 1930s, he made his way to Philadelphia where he met and married his first wife with whom he fathered two sons. Unfortunately the marriage ended in divorce. Although I never met her, my aunts and others always insisted that his wife had been mean-spirited and abusive and had taken his sons away from him in spite.

Once again life had dealt him a painful blow from which he would have to heal and find a way forward. And he did. In 1947, he married my Mama – Dorothy May Tabb Green – also a divorced parent of four children. From their union came me and my two younger brothers. Mama always told me how Daddy had asked her how she felt about having a child for him so that he could have a child to watch grow and to nurture. She agreed, and a year later I was born.

Now you might think that having had such a rough road to travel through childhood into adulthood, Daddy would have been cynical, or bitter or resigned in his view of life. He was not. He might have walled off his heart and emotions so as to protect himself from the next blows that life would surely deliver. He did not.

Instead, Daddy loved without reservation and with his whole heart – a heart that he wore on his sleeve for all to see. Perhaps because of his deprived childhood, Daddy had a special concern for young people. I can still see him standing in the door on the days he was home, encouraging the high schoolers who walked past our house on the way to Douglass High School. One of them actually came to show Daddy his diploma and to thank him. The young man explained that he had been ready to drop out, but because of Daddy's encouragement and offer to help anyway that he could, he had finished and was now a high school graduate. That was just how Daddy was with young folks.

Instead of cynicism or resignation, Daddy lived in hope. I know because Daddy had one saying that permeated his faith and punctuated his advice and counsel to any and everyone; and it gave him what he needed to move forward in spite of life's obstacles and challenges. His advice: "Keep on going, child, because 'tis better further on."

Daddy was not a physically imposing man – standing about 5'8" tall and weighing about 240 pounds, but as do most dads to their daughters, he seemed larger than life to me. I almost never heard him raise his voice to yell at us, and he always had time to listen to us and/or tell us wonderful stories about life in the country. I was convinced there was nothing he did not know and nothing he could not do; and most of all, I rested in the complete assurance that no harm would ever come near me as long as he lived. So sheltered and protected did Daddy keep me from the world that I was literally grown before I came to discover that there really were mean and evil people in the world who could and would do great harm to others just because they had the power to do so. Daddy couldn't understand meanness, and I remember him shedding tears as he heard tales of someone inflicting harm on another for absolutely no good reason.

My Daddy was a man of strong faith and his faith more than anything shaped his living and his loving. I don't know when he became a preacher, but during my early years he served as a co-pastor of a small church in downtown Baltimore. To the church he was Rev. Borum and to our neighbors and the stevedore gang with which he worked at Sparrows Point, he was "Reb."

He was an old-school conservative Baptist from the south who was uncompromising in his convictions. This meant that life in our home was a very different experience from that of our peers and playmates. For example: No liquor allowed in the house under any circumstances; Sunday was the Lord's day meaning Sunday School, church and family dinner with everyone seated at the table. This would be followed by family time which usually involved us hearing more stories about his and Mama's lives as they grew up on the country, or gathering around the old upright piano to sing the great old hymns of the church while Daddy plunked along on the keys as best he could.

Other convictions: Going to movies or shows on the Lord's Day was unthinkable. Daddy also saw dancing as "shaking yourself around for the devil." Women should not wear pants unless they had a job that required pants for the sake of preserving their modesty; women should not wear make-up ("war paint" in his words) because it ruined the natural beauty with which he believed every woman had been graced by God.

Sounds pretty severe doesn't it? There were many days I couldn't understand or appreciate his convictions. Like most young people, I wanted to be like my peers – do what they did; go where they went; say the things they said. In my youthful wisdom, Daddy's convictions seemed to be just a way to stop me from having any fun in life.

But the truth is, our home was anything but austere and joyless. It was full of energy, love, and laughter. Daddy was always doing something – building some project in his little tool room in the basement; trying out a new recipe for rhubarb pie in the kitchen; or studying the architectural designs for the house he dreamed of building "from the ground up;" tending his rose garden with such loving care that many people came to admire its beauty and take pictures of the flowers; or roaring with laughter at our antics and those of our childhood friends- all of whom loved to hang out at our house. Now this last thing always mystified me because we were pretty poor, often having fried potatoes and onions with fatback and King's syrup sopped up with Mama's hot biscuits for dinner. Our friends, on the other hand, had steak and shrimp dinners at home, but they preferred to come to our house and eat with us. Sometimes, one friend in particular would bring soda as her contribution because we couldn't afford it. When I finally got up the nerve to ask a couple of my friends why they preferred our house, without hesitation they said, "Because your parents pay us attention; your father talks with us and listens to us and teaches us so many things – we just love being around him."

Neighbors and co-workers (even those who lived lives diametrically opposed to Daddy's) likewise seemed drawn to him. I cannot count how many times they came to "Reb" for counsel and advice when trouble arose in their camps. They knew they were always welcome in our home, and they knew that Daddy would offer them honesty, wisdom and Jesus. He would pray with them and send them off with his final instruction, "Don't give up, keep on going, because "tis better further on." His calm assurances made them believers and gave them what they needed to keep on keeping on.

Now much of what I have shared has been with understanding that evolved over the years, as I looked back at life with Daddy. But the little girl in me thinks most about the Daddy who ran behind my bike to stop me from falling when he took the training wheels off. I remember the Daddy who sat me in his lap in the window when I got scared in the thunderstorm – telling me there was nothing to fear because it was just God doing His work. To me Daddy was the one who gave me my first piano lesson while I sat with him at that old mahogany upright. Daddy was the one who cried with and for me when he found me broken-hearted or sad over some childhood hurt or some want that he lacked the means or the money to provide. So often with tears brimming in his eyes, he would assure me, "If Daddy could, Daddy would." But I always, always knew that as long I was close enough to slip my little hand into his big square hands, everything was going to be all right.

So many memories of Daddy – the hunter who brought home rabbit and squirrel that Mama skinned and cleaned and fried up with onions and smothered with gravy and served with her homemade rolls; the fisherman who brought home fresh fish that Mama fried or sometimes steamed with seasonings and served with salty bacon; the crabber who brought home a basket full of crabs to steam, one or two of which would get loose and send us children scurrying to protect our toes from their claws; the Trumpeter for God who demanded to know from the pulpit," How shall we escape if we neglect so great a salvation?"

So many precious memories of Daddy whom the Lord let me have for only 16 years. You see Daddy died on Mother's Day 1964 two months after my sixteenth birthday. I remember being so angry with God and being completely mystified as to how God could take my Daddy who was so loving and so good while He allowed others who were mean and abusive and neglectful to live on. I resented everyone who kept on living while my Daddy was lying in the grave.

Appropriately, it was Daddy himself who had given me what I needed to move on from that paralyzing grief and anger and to find joy and laughter and hope to continue to embrace life. For it was at Daddy's knee that I met Jesus. One day when I sat at his feet by the window in his and Mama's bedroom, he began to tell me that I had another Bertha who lived inside me. Only God could really see her, but she was living in there. And it was that Bertha who would live eternally with God if I just prayed and asked Him to forgive my sins and let Jesus come into my heart. Not long after explaining this to me, Daddy left the room and went downstairs to work on something. I determined that if this Bertha was in there, sooner or later she would make an appearance so that I could see her. So I stripped all my clothes off and sat on the seat of the old vanity that had the three paned mirrors that allowed the two side mirrors to be folded in so that you could simultaneously have three views of yourself at once. I waited and waited, but she never came out. Finally, I just knelt there by the seat and prayed for forgiveness – unsure of what exactly all my sins were – and asked Jesus to come and live in me. Something moved in me. I could neither understand nor explain it, but I knew that when I left that room that day, I was not alone. Jesus was somehow with me. And from that day on, I began to journey with Jesus. I told Him about my hopes and dreams and secret thoughts. I prayed before I took tests in school, and I trusted Him to make me successful. I was all of seven or eight years old, but I just *knew* He was with me.

So in the midst of my grief and anger, it was the Jesus to whom Daddy had introduced me so many years earlier, to whom I ultimately turned for comfort and healing.

Finally, and perhaps most precious of all my memories are the last words my Daddy ever spoke to me. About six hours or so before he died, Mama took us to the hospital to say goodbye. Much like Jacob did with his sons at the end of his life, Daddy spoke to each of his children in turn and told us what he saw in us and what he hoped for each of us in the future - even though he wouldn't be with us because he was going to be with the Lord.

To me he said, "I'm not worried about you because God has got you. You are going to have to help the boys know Jesus so that we can all be together in heaven. It's not going to be easy, but keep at it because I don't want my family circle broken in glory. You got a long way to go without me, but your mother will be with you. Don't give her a hard time because she's going to have to finish raising you all by herself. But my spirit will be near. God promised me. I want you to stay in school and finish getting your education; keep yourself clean; and most of all, stay with the people of God. God's people will help you make the rest of this journey. And when it gets hard sometimes, don't give up; keep on because I promise you, 'tis better further on. I love you. You are the only little girl I've got. And with that we shared hugs and kisses with Daddy and left the hospital. Several hours later Mama came home and told us he was gone.

In the 50 years since, my brothers and I have continued to be guided by Daddy's faith and wisdom and counsel – often making life choices and decisions based on what Daddy would or would not have approved of. We have learned and lived the truth of his admonition, "Don't give up; keep on keeping on because tis better further on."

'Down on my knees'

By Rev. Felecia Diane Diggs, daughter of Richard McGuire Diggs

"Down on my knees when troubles rise,
I go to Jesus beyond the skies.
He promised me he would hear my plea
if I would tell him down on my knees."

My earliest recollection of the man known as Richard McGuire Diggs or Bubba, as his siblings called him, my father, was when I was three or four years of age. As we often did, my parents, my older sister and I went to the beach (we were almost surrounded by water, so it was easy to find a beach in those days.) I remember my father carrying me in his arms to the water but to avoid getting my feet wet, I used them to push myself up his chest. (I had a fear of water then and now.) Daddy did not force me into the water but over time he would help me become acclimated to being in it. I realized later that my father had shown himself to be my protector. There were many other times that also reinforced that thought.

For example, one night when I was supposed to be asleep I heard my mother tell my father she heard a potential intruder outside the house. I was probably school age by then. My father quietly got a small "reinforcement" and went to investigate the situation.

Fortunately, he didn't find anyone, but he made me again feel protected and safe. I felt he could handle anything that threatened me or my family.

On another occasion, when I was very young, my Dad sat me on the back of one of the two horses my grandfather had at the time. Her name was Lady and she was the gentler of the two. Standing directly beside Lady was Prince, who was known to be somewhat mean. He turned his head towards me and immediately my Dad removed me from Lady's back, seeing that I was terrified of Prince. Suffice it to say, I learned to be confident that regardless of where I was, if Daddy was close by, my world would be a safe and secure place.

The mention of horses might make you think I grew up on a farm, and I pretty much did since my grandfather's house was only a stone's throw from ours. Not only did he have a few horses prior to my arrival, he also had a few cows and chickens. Papa, as we called him, made his living farming the land and selling tomato plants, sweet potato sprouts, eggs, flowers and more. I remember how people would come during the summer to pick strawberries. I even helped him to water his plants as a young girl. (I felt like a big girl when I graduated from using the bucket and dipper to using the sprinkler can.) We had string beans, egg plant, sweet potatoes and tomatoes, not to mention the watermelon, apples, pears, walnuts and my favorite, damson plum preserves. I omitted my not-so-favorite, mulberries and persimmons. Since my father was his youngest son, Papa and my Dad worked closely together. They formed more than one location to produce and sell soybeans and corn. I recall how Daddy would pull the planter, plows and combine with his tractor, (by now the horses were gone) and my grandfather would fertilize the plants as he drove along behind him. Sometimes, Dad would ride my younger sister and me on the side of the tractor. That was an idyllic life to me at the time, until I realized my summer vacations weren't as elaborate and pristine as my other young classmates. (We were asked to talk about our summer vacations in class.)

Although an auto mechanic by trade, my Dad was also a farmer throughout his life. He even let me and my sisters (there were three of us by then) have, what we thought was, a pet pig once. We named him Arnold and took delight in feeding him and watching him grow. Little did we kids know that there was some other purpose for Arnold than being our pet. When we realized my father had the intention of making him part of our meal also, the three of us cried. Though parting was a bitter sorrow, when my Mom presented him on the table, we soon got over it.

Although my father only completed six grades of school, I knew he was quite intelligent and could accomplish almost anything. Why would I think this? Growing I witnessed doing many things from throwing horseshoes to pulling someone's car out of a ditch to hunting squirrel and rabbit to marching and carrying the U.S. flag in a parade. As a veteran of World War II, he was a member of the American Legion and marched as part of the color guard.

While witnessing Daddy doing many things, I learned some of his favorite things. My father liked horses and cars more than a little bit. Telling stories was another favorite of his. I remember him telling me more than one horse story. The following story had me listening to every word and inflection. Let me say first that when he was a young boy, having an automobile to transport you places was rare for Blacks. So there were horses and wagons or buggies that took you to church and the market. For my grandfather there were special Sunday go-to-meeting horses and other horses for riding or pulling a plow. My father was told that he should not play around with this one special horse. One day he and his male cousin wanted to race on horseback. (I'm sure it wasn't the only time this happened.) My father decided to try out the exact horse he had been forbidden to ride. The race course had a downward slope right before a sharp curve. As they were traveling at break-neck speed, Daddy came to the curve and couldn't quite make it. Instead, he continued straight into a swampy area. Not only did he race the wrong horse, but got the horse covered with mud! No problem. He would simply wash the horse off and put him in the barn where he belonged. The bath did not cover up the fact that he had been ridden and my grandfather let him know as much. "Bubba, didn't I tell you not to ride that horse?" Knowing that he was due a lashing with a long strap, my Dad ran into the woods and stayed until dark. Fearing the dark as much his father's strap, he sneaked into the house when he thought his father had gone to bed. His punishment was delayed until the next day but his mother came to his rescue this time.

When he could get the money to purchase them, Daddy possessed several cars as a young man. I believe a part of why he would always have a car is that he was skilled and creative at repairing them. He apprenticed (unofficially) under an older mechanic who also provided him with a paid job at his auto garage when he was a teenager. He continued to teach himself and pick up auto repairing skills through a series of jobs until he retired from the Naval Weapon Station in Williamsburg, Va.

I am sure a definite benefit of my Dad being able to keep and repair cars as a young man was being able to date my mother. When he got permission to take my mother out, he would also have to take several of her sisters with them. My father eventually built himself a garage where he could work on automobiles at home. There was never a time during my school age years that I remember my father not owning at least two cars at a time. He always had a spare one in case someone else in the family needed one. Nor do I remember there not being 2-3 cars at our home at once for Daddy to diagnose or repair. Sometimes, usually on a Saturday morning, my father would ask me if I wanted to help him work on some brakes. Of course in my mind, I said "No, of course not. It was Saturday and I didn't have to go to school and planned to sleep late." However, while asking me he would rub or pat my head and flash me a big smile, so I couldn't tell him "No." The way he asked for my help or cooperation melted me and I hated to disappoint him.

I don't know how many years my father worked as a mechanic, but he became so good at it that he could diagnose a problem from a distance and without seeing the car. For that reason and others, I had friends who began to call him Dr. Diggs.

As I mentioned before, my father freely shared stories of his youth and young adult life. Unlike many veterans, he didn't mind talking about where he had served during World War II from the type of tasks he performed to the people he met along the way. He also shared how he was very ill the latter part of his two or so years in the military. He came home with a diagnosis of kidney disease. I am so glad that God healed him of that illness! The doctors also predicted that due to his suffering with mumps as an adult male, he would most likely not be able to have children. Well, surprise, surprise! He ended up having three daughters with my mother and never acted as if he regretted not having any boys. Daddy always made each of us girls feel like we were wanted and special.

Another humorous story he told about his youth was going fishing with his father. Once, the story goes, the two of them went out in a little dingy of a boat to fish. My father began to notice the clouds gathering and the sky becoming dark. He told his father that it looked like a squall (storm) was coming. Papa kept fishing and said nothing. The signs of an impending storm became more profound to my father - the sky had become very dark and the water was getting a bit rougher. So he said again to his father "Papa, I think we're about to have a storm." His father kept on fishing. Suddenly it began to rain and the boat started rocking because of the choppy water. Before my Dad could say any more, he had been thrown overboard. Somehow he and his father made it back to shore, but my Dad was really shaken by the experience. After all, he thought he could have drowned. When he arrived home, he went immediately to his mother and said, "Mamma, Papa tried to kill me out there!" I am not sure if he and his father went fishing again, but most likely they did.

Besides almost drowning as a young boy, Dad was kicked in the side of his head by a horse, which caused a mild hearing loss; In addition, as a young man, he had a few mishaps involving his cars. It seems that my father loved milk and drank it about every day. When he would come in the house after having a hard day's work, he would ask one of his sisters to give him a glass of milk. She would oblige (in exchange for using his car) by serving him a big glass of warm milk. Since milk relaxed him and often helped him go to sleep, that and driving a car were a bad combination. Several of his auto accidents were caused by him falling asleep at the wheel, though none were too serious. (It is my suspicion that my father had undiagnosed sleep apnea. If so, we shared that malady.)

I began this chapter with a verse from an old song, "Down on My Knees," which was sung in the 1950s by quartettes. This song is very important to me, since the second verse of the song was one of the last things my father taught me and sang with me. By this time he was 90 and had been diagnosed with Alzheimers. The other reason I began with this verse is to suggest how important music was to my father. He loved to sing and that is another memory I have of him throughout my life. To my knowledge, he sang with at least two quartettes and one or two men's choruses.

His debut gig singing on the radio station came when he was a member of the *Kings of Jubilee*. This group sang every Sunday morning (strictly voluntary) on the local station. I am not aware of how long this a cappella group existed but members of the group stayed in touch long after the group disbanded. The *Humming Jubilee Chorus* was the next group he sang with, which was very similar to the first. In this group Daddy sang along side a couple of his brothers-in-law, as his father-in-law played guitar. What a joy it was to me that many of the rehearsals were in our home. With his smooth and melodious tenor, my father sang lead on many songs but also harmonized well. It seemed that most of my childhood, Dad was singing with this group; it was evident that he enjoyed it immensely.

The musical surprise he presented to me was after I was an adult. I discovered at that time that my father could play the harmonica very well! Why this was a secret during my childhood, one can only guess. Perhaps, he sang so much, he didn't have time or the right circumstance didn't present itself. It may have been that my mother had heard enough of it by the time we children came along (not that she didn't sing as well). The reason that makes the most sense to me is the noise of three young girls was more than enough for both of my parents. After we got a piano in the house, plus a few other instruments, does one have to guess why he didn't pull out one of several harmonicas? One of my fondest memories, however, was when my Dad and I performed a duet for a Black History celebration – he played harmonica and I played guitar and sang. We were a hit!

Music definitely was always a part of life in the Diggs home. Another aspect of life and my father's character is reflected in the first line of the song, "Down on my knees …" Even though it could be a very private thing, I also observed my father praying many times in public. Thanking and calling on the name of his heavenly Father was something he seemed to do easily. His relationship with the Father seemed one of quietness and peace at times, yet of confidence and boldness at other times.

It was obvious to me that my father was talented and skillful in more than one area of his life. In addition, one trait of his that shouted out to me (and does even now that he is gone) was his natural way of showing kindness to others. I can say I never witnessed him being unkind when someone had a need or asked for help. He, along with my mother, went out of his way in showing kindness. I will never forget the time when snow was on the ground, it was very cold and my Dad had come into the house to rest for the evening. He received a call that a neighbor had slipped into a ditch and was stuck in the snow. Dad left his warm house and comfortable recliner to go out again into the cold to pull someone out of a snow bank. No money was exchanged; a simple "thank-you" was enough. Other times, he would go underneath a cold building to remedy a heating problem or after working all day, work late into the evening to start someone's car that had stopped working. There are countless times when I observed this type of selfless act. He just couldn't help himself. Besides singing and showing kindness to others, the other time my father would exude this type of joy was watching his three girls get up on Christmas morning to discover happiness!

Dad was 93 when he went home to be with his heavenly Father. Although he ceased carrying on regular conversations with me and was only mobile when being pushed in a wheelchair, Dad's temperament remained the same. As before his illness, he was calm, pleasant and cooperative with his caregivers. Even then, I knew I had been blessed with the best father in the world.

A hard working dad

By Bettie Crest Durant, daughter of Eddie Owens Crest

My dad, Eddie Owens Crest, was born in 1913 in rural
North Carolina. He was a sharecropper and lived on a
farm with his wife, Luvenia and their seven children. As
a tenant farmer he shared a portion of the crops he raised
with the owner of the land on which he lived. Dad spent
his days in the fields since large crops of cotton and
tobacco made for long hours and back-breaking work.
Mom took care of the house, making a home and raising
the children. In May of 1957 when my oldest brother
William graduated from high school, he moved to
Baltimore, Maryland where he lived with relatives. Later
that year, in December, my dad moved the rest of the
family to Baltimore where two more children were born.
We became part of the Great Northward Migration of the
1900s where millions of African Americans moved from
the rural south to cities of the northeastern, midwestern
and western United States.
In Baltimore, Dad found work as a construction worker.
He was always a hard worker and was used to working
with his hands. He enjoyed construction work and loved
putting up new buildings and working on existing
structures. He worked on the construction of several
buildings in downtown Baltimore including the
Blaustein Building and the Garmatz Federal Office
Building. Dad also worked on the construction of the
Jones Falls Expressway.

Construction work could be hard to find at times,
depending on the weather, but even in the worst of times

I can't ever remember being hungry with no prospect of another meal coming soon. We did receive state assistance at times and had many a meal with welfare cheese, powdered milk, spam or canned beef. But it was not always that way. Times got better when the rest of the country did better. Dad went to work every day that he could. If he wasn't sick he went and looked and found work whether steady or part-time. My brother Rufus remembers going along when Dad went out with his friend Mr. Charlie who sold fruit from the back of his truck during the summer. We were well fed and well cared for.

I remember Dad taking us shopping on Gay Street in east Baltimore. There was a store called the Gay Kiddie Shop where we got shoes and clothes when we were young children. Sometimes, but not often, Dad took us "downtown." It was a special trip and treat to go shopping in downtown Baltimore on Lexington Street. We might even stop to buy hot dogs or peanuts from street vendors or from the Grants Department Store lunch counter. Sometimes Dad would point upwards, and looking up I would see hundreds of birds, pigeons I guess, perched neatly along the edges of the tall buildings. Dad held my hand firmly as we walked along the sidewalks downtown, with me skipping a little to keep up with his long strides, so I would not get lost or left behind. One result of those trips was that I learned how to walk fast and that became my normal way of walking. As I grew up, my friends always complained that I walked too fast whenever we walked together.

Daddy liked to walk. Having lived in rural areas of North Carolina where everything was far apart, he was used to walking long distances. I think living in the city could be somewhat confining and he felt a need to get out and stretch his legs, so he walked around the neighborhoods.

In his sixties Dad had a massive heart attack resulting in quadruple by-pass surgery. After a stay in the hospital and the proper amount of recuperation time, Dad resumed his walking regimen. Later, when we moved to east 36th Street, we were just a block from Memorial Stadium, home of the Baltimore Orioles and the Baltimore Colts. Dad would often walk around the entire stadium and parking lot. On some days he continued on to Lake Montebello, a city reservoir about six blocks from the stadium. There were bike and walking lanes there. Dad would walk the distance around the lake, about a mile and a quarter, and then back home, a combined distance of at least two and a half to three miles.

Mom would accompany him sometimes, but she later stopped going. She said he walked too fast.

My dad was, what I like to call, a character. He loved to talk about, well, almost anything! He enjoyed telling stories about his family and friends, his life on the farm in North Carolina, about work on construction sites in Baltimore City, and even about people he met or saw on the transit bus or street car. He would explain the intricacies of constructing a building floor by floor, from digging the hole with huge pieces of construction equipment, to laying the cement base for the bottom floor, to how the scaffolding was put up where the

33

workmen stood to build the upper floors. He and his
buddies from the neighborhood would gather in the
house at the dining room table or, in the warmer months
on the front steps or in the backyard drinking beer, and
tell life tales for hours. We children were usually outside
playing or in the house upstairs.

But my brother Warren remembers one time when he
was not outside or upstairs.
Daddy was with his buddies and Warren, watching them,
decided that beer must be really good, so he began
asking dad if he could have some. Of course Dad said
"No," but Warren continued to ask over and over again,
and actually threw a tantrum when he couldn't get his
way. Finally, Dad, thinking to teach my brother a lesson,
poured some beer in a cup and told Warren he had to
drink all of it. Warren took a couple of healthy swallows
and promptly spit it all out! Whereupon my dad then
expressed his displeasure with my brother for wasting
perfectly good beer that Warren had been told he
shouldn't have in the first place. Warren didn't sit down
comfortably for a couple of hours but hasn't, to this day,
drunk another drop of beer!

Dad was a family man. He loved his family and enjoyed
spending quality time with his wife and children. Our
cousin, Leon, had an Oldsmobile 88 and the family
would pile into his car and go to Arundel's ice cream
parlor for a Sunday afternoon treat.
Dad loved the grandchildren and much to the surprise of
his children, he enjoyed holding them-until they cried.
He would take the toddlers on short walks and loved
making toys for them. For some reason Dad called his

male grandchildren odd names like "Bill Datsun" when they were little. Two of my nephews, William and Travis (Warren's sons), got the names Blister and Fiddle. I don't remember who had which nickname and I have no idea where any of those names came from.
He didn't have any for the girls.

In our home, every child went to school every day. Dad was very proud when we received our diplomas. He was especially proud of Sarah, the youngest girl and the last child to be born in North Carolina. She was the first to graduate college and to get a masters degree. When Dad was in the hospital, he used to brag to the doctors that his daughter taught at the university and they could ask her questions if they needed to know something. The doctors were amused. My sister was embarrassed.

My Dad was a praying man. He had great faith in God. We all went to church on Sunday, so on a Saturday night Dad would trim the boys' hair and sometimes neighbors brought their sons for Dad to cut their hair also.
My brothers, nephews and my son all have stories to tell about Daddy cutting their hair. They all agree that Dad's hands were so big he could place the palm of his hand on the top of their head, fingers spread to the sides and front and, basically, move their heads around much like a person moves the gears when driving a stick shift. And you didn't dare move your head, especially when he came near your ears and neck with his clippers!

Daddy was a fixer-upper. He loved to figure out what made a thing stop working and fix it or find or make a new part for something with an obvious defect. This often meant taking a thing apart to see how it's made and how it's supposed to function.

I remember the time my sister Sarah and I were having trouble with our washing machine so we came to our parents' house to do laundry. The handle on the laundry basket broke. Now, this was a plain old plastic laundry basket that could be gotten from the "5 and dime" or, now-a-days, from the dollar store or Walmart. But anyway, Dad took that basket out in the back yard to see what could be done with it. About an hour later, he brought the basket back. He had put two steel rods along both sides of that plastic laundry basket and secured them with twine. Needless to say, that basket lasted another 5 or 6 years until we just got tired of using it. The thing was, when you put a load of wet clothes in that steel-rodded laundry basket, you almost needed a lever and pulley to lift it!

My niece, Mylika, tells of the time her granddaddy fixed her curling iron.

Mylika had complained, within earshot of her grandfather, that her curling iron wasn't working properly-when it worked at all. Well, one day she came downstairs, complained bitterly about her curling iron, then left for school. When she returned home around 3:30 p.m., upon entering the dining room she stopped short, frozen in shock. There on the dining room table, in about 417 pieces (according to her) was her curling iron, separated neatly into each of its component parts. "Granddaddy!!?? "Oh no!" Mylika was horrified.

Dad, in an effort to calm her, began repeating, "I'll fix it. I'll fix it."

Mylika, thinking she would never be able to use her curling iron again, turned and rushed from the room. Later that evening there was a knock on her bedroom door. Upon answering Mylika was presented with her curling iron-all in one piece! My dad handed it to her, nodded his head, turned and left. The next morning, Mylika used her curling iron before school as usual and continued to use it for another 2 years. She was very grateful to her granddaddy. My Dad loved fixing things, and more often than not, they worked.

Now, Dad was a picker-upper as well as a fixer-upper. On his walks around the neighborhood, he would see broken or abandoned pieces of furniture, toys, tools, or household items and would bring home anything he thought had the potential to be rebuilt or repaired and restored to usefulness. My Mom complained about Dad bringing junk home.
Some things turned out quite well. We have a small child's rocking chair that Dad found and brought home one day. Mom complained about it but when Dad started to work on it, Mom joined him and together they restrung the seat with twine and cleaned and varnished the back and legs and rockers. That chair sits in the living room and is loved and used by grand and great-grand children to this day.

My dad was very particular about the work he did and he was that way about himself as well. Whatever he worked on, he would labor over it until it was what he considered the best it could be. He was the same way when he dressed, especially for church and special events. He always wore suits to church, three piece suits preferably and he always wore a hat. His shirt and tie and pocket square had to match. Sometimes he even gave Mom advice on her outfit. Whenever we took Dad shopping to buy new clothes, if he bought a suit he especially liked, he would always proclaim, "Guess you can bury me in this one." He had at least four suits that we were told we could bury him in. As it turned out, Dad, being a member of the Senior Usher Board at our church, New Metropolitan Baptist Church in west Baltimore, was buried in his white three-piece usher's uniform with white shoes, white gloves, yellow tie and hanky. No hat.

Dad loved church. As well as ushering, he taught Sunday School and worked in the

Bread of Life Food Ministry. We were all as proud as he when Rev. Richard Dickens presented him with a certificate for outstanding service for his work in the food ministry.

But, speaking of hats, one of daddy's favorite headpieces was not a hat but a cap. His Baltimore Orioles baseball cap. Dad loved baseball. Living just a block from the stadium, he would take his transistor radio out into the backyard and get set up with food and a can of beer and listen to the game. He would get extra sound effects from the actual noise at the stadium, especially if there was a home room or a close play or a disputed call by the umpire. Sometimes when watching the game on TV, he would turn the sound down on the TV and listen to the play-by-play on the radio.

My Dad enjoyed the simple life but he was a curious, interested, and interesting individual. In his lifetime he saw so many changes and new things come to be, such as computers and the Internet, manned space flight, microwave ovens, cardiac pacemakers, television and later, color television. He was particularly interested in the building of the World Trade Center in New York in the 1960s-1970s.

Dad also used to like us to drive him down 95 south towards BWI Airport and we'd watch planes take off and land. We would ride around the waterfront before it became the Baltimore Inner Harbor. We did visit the Inner Harbor many times. We got to see the Tall Ships at dock. We drove through downtown and Dad would point out buildings he'd help to put up. He was very proud of the work he'd done on the tall buildings.

Dad believed in working for a living and earning your pay, and that is what he taught his children. We all were expected to get jobs when we finished school. Dad did not graduate high school, but he made sure that every one of his children understood the value of education. He could not afford it, so we would have to work our way through college if we didn't get scholarships. No one stayed home idle. He said the Bible says if a man "don't work, he don't eat." Dad believed and lived by those words and he made sure we understood and obeyed them as well.

In his latter years when he couldn't work or walk as much as he used to, Dad watched a lot of TV. He always followed the Orioles but he had a few favorite shows he liked to watch: Walker, Texas Ranger, McGyver, Perry Mason, The Andy Griffith Show, I Love Lucy, Gunsmoke, Bonanza and Wagon Train, to name a few.

He had a garden in the backyard. He grew string beans, cabbage, tomatoes, and collard greens.

Daddy passed away in May of 2001, just four months before the bombing of the World Trade Center on September 11. I'm glad he didn't see that, though we hated to lose him. But I can just imagine how sad, yet fascinated, he would have been to see those towers come down the way that they did. He would have spent hours wondering and offering possible explanations to anyone within earshot, about how those buildings must have been constructed.

I'm so very proud of my dad.
He had no diploma, yet he valued his knowledge.
He had no title, yet he valued himself as a person.

My Dad, Eddie Owens Crest:
He worked hard. He rested well.
He loved his family. He enjoyed his friends.
He believed his God.

Daddy and Me

By Tiffany Christina Ginyard, daughter of David
Michael Ginyard

Sugar Bear. My Daddy's nickname for me. At 34, I still
get warm inside when he calls me that. It takes me back
to the nights he came home after work with a Colt 45
and a good mood. He would turn on some smooth jazz,
extend his hand for me to join him on our living room
dance floor. I'd step up on his feet and he'd sweep me
away into a daddy-daughter dance that I wished he could
make last forever.

***

I remember vividly the nights he'd give me bubble baths.
He'd say, "When you start looking like a California
Raisin, it's time to get out." After I got out of the tub,
brushed my teeth and put on my underclothes, my father
would be waiting for me in my room with some Suave
lotion and before putting on the night clothes he neatly
laid out for me, he would lotion my whole body down.
The strength of his hands come to me as I write this. He
massaged my body so intensely. He was so careful with
me. I felt so secure. He tended to crevices of my fingers
and toes, polishing the ash from elbows...

***

My father makes the best breakfasts. His eggs taste like
pure love. To this day, he makes these overstuffed
omelettes with bacon and sausage and at least two types
of cheese. My daddy loves cheese. And so do I. I didn't
look forward to dinners as much because he was always
making some vegetable my taste buds rejected. "Make

sure you eat your vegetables, Sugar Bear." He was Popeye the Sailor Man when it came down to his spinach and mixed vegetables. I remember plenty nights I faked sick, asked to be excused from the table and went to the bathroom to spit out chewed up veggies I had pretended to swallow. I sometimes wonder if he had stayed longer, would I have acquired a taste for veggies other than broccoli and collard greens. Would I still like omelettes? I mean, I still like them, but I rarely think to order them from a menu or cook them myself, because honestly, only my Daddy's will do.

***

My father drove a smoke grey 1992 Ford Taurus. The interior was blood red. Perfectly round polka dots from his Newports were burnt into the driver's seat. One time he plucked an ash out the window and it boomeranged back into the car through the back window hazing his shirt and burning his back. All I can do is shake my head and laugh; as I write this I can still see him pouncing about in his seat, in pain and surprise, trying to brush his shoulders off. He maintained control of the car, steering it with his knee. To a 6-year-old tomboy diva like myself, driving with no hands was awesome. For that, my father was "the man" to me. Riding in the car with my Dad as a child was an adventure. He was the first person to introduce me to driving.

We lived one block over from the main street in our neighborhood. Whenever my father turned off the main street onto a byway leading to the street where we lived, he would look over his shoulder to the back seat and pose, "You going to take us…?"

I would jump out of my seat belt and into his lap before the word "home" rolled off his tongue. It was our thing. He'd pull the car over and set me between his skinny legs--my toes were nowhere near the floor--and let me steer the car up the street. That always made me feel like a "big girl."

I was thrilled he trusted my little self to steer the wheel all by myself. But then again, I'd always known my father to be amazingly in tune with the road-- and me. So, I never doubted myself, or entertained the thought of crashing into something. My Daddy wouldn't allow it; he did have total control over the pedals the whole time. Nevertheless, I could feel the effort he put into empowering me with a sense of independence. He talked me calmly through every maneuver. Maybe he was so relaxed because he sensed I had a natural affinity for the open road too, or, more realistically, he was scared out of his wits, but being courageous for his baby girl.

***

A hurricane hit my home back in the late 90s. It was an isolated storm. It just hit the basement where my Daddy stayed, but it rocked the entire house to its core. The basement was more than a man cave; it's where my father lived for as long as I can remember, so I was devastated to come home one day to discover that a twister had ravaged his room, leaving behind only remnants of a life.

From what I gathered from eavesdropping on their arguments, I knew deep down inside there'd come a time when Mommy and Daddy would call it quits. They lived separate lives within the house all my life. I thought that

43

was normal. I knew of no intimacy between them; I could probably count on my hand the times I'd seen them kiss or hug. So when the time came for them to divorce, a word that wasn't in my elementary school vocabulary yet, I was at a lost for words. Whatever it meant, I never imagined it involved him leaving our home. I would say that was the first storm, of many, to blow through my little life, leaving my head spinning and my heart choked up for years to come.

Daddy was gone with the wind, and there I was, lost in my own home, not knowing where to even begin to find him. Lisa Stanfield's, "Been around the world, and I, I, I, can't find my baby," would become a cut on the soundtrack of my childhood story. It was a melody that resonated with me so deeply that it made me sad, and gave me hope at the same time. I hoped that I'd someday reclaim the love the storm so suddenly stole from me.

My first love affair was short-lived, and I felt short-changed. By the time I entered adolescence, he and I barely knew each other any more. As time went on, our relationship withered like a rose left in a beautiful vase on the table of a dark room. Weekend visits dwindled to holidays and special occasions like a fashion show, an award ceremony or a funeral. I'll admit, until recently, I was a little numb, I was harboring hurt. Angry and resentful. But at times, I would reason with myself that he was only a phone call away, which was more than what many of my peers could say. There were times I'd remember to be grateful that I wasn't a fatherless child. But still I wondered (and I did a little wandering too) well into young adulthood, what it would have been like if the storm had never come.

Every time I started missing my Daddy I would write. A poem. A journal entry. A love letter. Not necessarily to him; but anything to cheer myself up, to numb myself from missing him. From thinking about him. From being mad at him. Writing, no matter the subject matter, kept the bitterness and unforgiveness at bay. Here lately, though, memories of the first seven years of my life-- when my father was front and center--have been the subject of my musings, and it has aroused in me a profound sense of gratitude that over the course of seven years I had the opportunity to develop a strong sense of who my father truly is and that he loved me. Writing has created a safe space for me to honor the little girl in me who knows with all her heart, that David Michael Ginyard, is and always will be my first love.

Writing about the memories have gradually healed me. The process of recording the most intimate moments I had with my father has opened up so much space in my heart to love, not just him, but myself, unconditionally.

I know he didn't really mean to start a new life, with a new woman and her children. But still I didn't understand it. So life between then and now has been trying to make sense of it all.

I never doubted his love for a second

By Dr. Lynda Byrd Logan, daughter of James Edward Byrd Jr.

Initially, I thought writing about my relationship with my father would be easy. It wasn't until I started to revisit my life as the daughter of James Edward Byrd Jr. that the complexity of the man and the relationship began to weigh me down. I am a lot like my father in temperament and outlook. Neither of us ever wanted to do harm, but neither did we suffer fools gladly. We were both comfortable in our own company, my father reading the news and sports and me reading Jane Austen and Dickens.

Believe it or not, my father introduced me to Jane Austen, Charles Dickens, Willa Cather and Laura Ingles Wilder and a host of other authors when I was only about five years old. He didn't read them, but he bought their books for me. We could sit together for hours and never say a word to each other. The silences were never strained. We disliked all the same people and things—with the exception of National Bohemian Beer and liver and onions, which he loved and I could not abide. I'm not terribly social and neither was he. He would accompany my mother to cookouts and gatherings at the homes of her friends, but it was always under duress. The only social gathering he routinely attended was watching the Baltimore Colts play football with the other Bench Warmers, Uncle Jim, Mr. Leo, Charles Bowers and a few others. The wives always fixed these high cholesterol, high carb, high sugar, artery hardening half-time meals that they served while the guys argued over the likely outcome of the game. On those Sundays when the games were played in the old Memorial Stadium on 33rd Street, they had season tickets and sat out in the cold eating hotdogs, drinking beer and impressing each other with their knowledge of the game. Or not.

He and I had a standing date every Saturday morning from the time I was potty-trained until I was about 12 years old. It was the highlight of my week because I enjoyed the comradery. I didn't have to explain why I preferred reading to TV or hopscotch. To him, I was normal. In hindsight, both of us were a tad off the beam. I remember sitting with him in the Waverly Laundromat on one of those Saturday outings and lamenting about the fact that the initials of the names of my siblings all spelled a readable word (JEB, REB, DAB) but mine did not (LFB). He said, "Your initials are pronounced Lufaba." So of course, I challenged him to pronounce his mother's initials, SFBBF. He didn't bat an eye, just said "Sufabubufa, Suf for short." Yes, he was definitely three bricks short of a load. It's interesting that for all the time I spent with him, I can't say I really knew him. He rarely talked about himself and much of what I have gleaned about his life and loves is from other people's perception of him.

His younger sisters, Ruth and Naomi—my grandmother had a religious, steeped-in-the-word-of-God bent—adored him. In their eyes, he could do no wrong. They were forever telling me stories about his exploits as the elder brother of two—if not exactly wild—out there sisters. Evidently, he was not as devout as his mother and contrived all kinds of scenarios where they could skip some of their church appearances—Tuesday night, junior choir rehearsal; Wednesday night, prayer meeting; Thursday night, Bible study; Friday night, youth gathering, and of course, two services on Sunday. I know they speak truth because I will never forget the time that Mt. Zion had some sort of appreciation service for his mother. I call it the funeral with a live corpse. There sat Grandma Sue in a huge high-backed chair on the pulpit and a parade of preachers and church lay leaders from the DMV region paid tribute to her for lifelong service to the Baptist Convention. I was sitting next to my father and he passed me a note that said, "When I give the signal, put your hand over your mouth as if you are ill." So, he gave the signal, I pretended to be ill, and he scooped me up and ran out of the church. We went to Highs and got ice cream. Neither my grandmother nor my mother were happy campers. I thought I had just died and gone to heaven.

I remember another time when a Jehovah's Witness came to the door to talk about their particular brand of religion. My father opened the door and before they could get a word in edgewise, he asked, "Don't you all have any young pretty girls that you can send out? All I seem to get are the old and ugly ones." Although I never actually, saw them do it, I think the Witnesses painted the lintel with the blood of goats, because from that point on no Witness ever knocked on our door again.

He never said an unkind word to me or about me in my hearing. I never heard him say that he loved me or anyone. Somehow, he communicated to me that I was loved. I never doubted it for a second. It wasn't until he died that I found out how much my mother resented the fact that I could get him to do things just by asking when she could not. She used to tell me to go ask my father to take us somewhere or to do something and I simply complied with her request. It never occurred to me that he would not have done something if she asked, but would do it for me. I did know on some level that my relationship with my mother was not as close as it was with my father.

There was one three-year period when he left home and went to live with his mother and unmarried, spinster sister, Ruth. Every Sunday, he would come to the house and get me and my two little brothers and take us to the Smithsonian or to see the Liberty Bell, or to Aberdeen Proving Grounds, or to Washington, D.C. to see the Cherry blossoms. I didn't pay much attention at the time but looking back I see that those outings were teaching moments. He made us read the little plaques at each exhibit and then quizzed us on the ride home. I have no idea what precipitated the move. I do remember that there was peace on Boone Terrace (really Boone Street—I had delusions of grandeur) while he was only visiting on Sunday. I also remember that he came every Friday night to give my mother money for the mortgage and groceries.

At the end of the semi-estrangement, he and my mother sat me and my brothers down to talk about my father coming to live with us again. I was about seven or eight at the time. I piped up and said that I voted "No." Life seemed more pleasant when he lived elsewhere. I couldn't identify the tension, I just knew things were tense when he lived in the household. He thought my "No" vote was funny, my mother not so much. My mother informed me that this meeting was for imparting information not taking a vote. So, he moved back in and life went on. I don't remember any recurrence of the tensions, but neither do I recall any warmth. We still went on outings on Sunday, but now my mother went along too.

He never missed a day from work in 35 years and even though he drank National Bo for breakfast, he never had an accident. How he managed that I cannot say. Once I asked him why he didn't use the turn signals. He replied that he knew where he was going, and it wasn't anybody else's business. That seemed a little strange to me, but he was Dad and I learned early on that he didn't have to make sense. Even though he didn't say a lot, he was definitely the adult authority in our household. My mother would holler at the top of her voice and we virtually ignored her. My father would give us a look and never open his mouth. We jumped to attention immediately. Why, I don't know because he never struck any of us or punished us in any way. I guess we thought that he would punish us if push came to shove.

One other peculiarity that I remember was sitting with him every evening while he ate his dinner. He didn't eat with us and I thought it was because he drove a truck for a living and had to make deliveries in D.C., Virginia and Pennsylvania. I was in junior high school when I found out that it was his practice to stop at the Garrett Lounge on his way home every evening. He'd have a few

National Bos sitting at the bar in solitary splendor. He would then get in his Ford, LTD and drive home, high as a kite. My mother would leave his dinner on the stove. He would combine everything into one pot, heat it and eat it. Even though the sight of it made me nauseous, I would sit there with him while he ate. Sometimes he would talk about something that was disturbing his ordered life. Other times he said nothing at all.

Once when I decided to take a tailoring class, he allowed me to use him as my model. I made a blue, corduroy suit. The man practically slept in that suit. I got tired of seeing him in it. He never said he was proud of my efforts, but he let me know that he appreciated something I had done for him. The one thing that he would routinely question me about was my grades. He never said "good job" or "keep up the good work" but the very fact that he asked made me know he expected and took pleasure in my doing well in school. I knew instinctively that he valued education and wanted me to go as far as I could in school. I suppose I went to college because I knew it would please him. In this regard, he and my mother were on the same page. They both thought it would be a good idea for a female to have something to fall back on if she got hitched to a no-good man. They felt that my brothers could always make a living, ditch digging if necessary, but a female had few options if she had no academic credential that would allow her to teach or be a nurse or a librarian.

I knew my mother was proud of the fact that my sister and I had gone to college. She would bring it up to strangers in the line at the grocery store. I didn't realize how proud my father was until I went to the Garrett Lounge to pick him up one day and he introduced me to the barflies as his daughter. Someone asked, "Which one are you, the teacher or the librarian?' Actually, he said 'libarian,' but I let that pass. Evidently, my father would say things about us to his drinking buddies that he did not voice to us.

The only time I have ever heard of him being angry enough to become argumentative was when I asked how I got my name. My elder sister had been named for my maternal grandmother—Anita Louise. Ergo, my paternal grandmother assumed I would be named Susan Frances, after her. My father objected to that rather strenuously. I think he had some rather severe mommy issues. At any rate, Grandma Sue was willing to compromise if they would let her pick the name. If my father couldn't live with Susan Frances, she wanted him to consider naming me Orangejean. Well, the argument raged for six weeks and I still didn't have a name. My father was in favor of Jay (who names a child Jay if her last name is Byrd?); My mother came down on the side of Susan Frances and my grandmother wanted Orangejean. There didn't seem to be any solution so Dr. Johnson, who was the neighborhood doc filled out the birth certificate, named me Lynda Frances, and told them once he had filed the certificate. Evidently, no one argued after that because for the past 69 years, I have been Lynda Frances.

The truly pitiful thing was that my grandmother never got over it. She would send me birthday cards addressed to Susan Frances or sometimes she would address them to Lynda but spell Lynda with an "i" instead of the "y." I would simply remove the cash and throw the envelop away. Again, I have no idea why naming me after his mother caused such angst for old James Edward, especially since it was only a few years after that that he left us and went to live with good old Susan Frances Booze Byrd Fuller.

Let me end with some of the pearls of wisdom that he did utter during the time I spent with him.
- ✓ Happiness is optional. You can choose to be happy and you should.
- ✓ There will always be people who want to call you n——r and all sorts of ugly names, but that does not make you whatever they call you.
- ✓ Some folk are in your life for a reason (serving on a committee together); some are there for a season (you have things in common and you hang out doing those things; very few people are in your life forever (family, best friend from childhood), so learn who is who and bring to the table only what is necessary for each relationship.
- ✓ I know if he were alive today, he would have this to say to our president, "Donald John, stop thinking; don't even let your mind wander; It's too small to be out by itself." He truly did not suffer fools gladly.

My favorite bit of advice was, when things go south, and they will, set your alarm clock for 15 minutes. Piss and moan and feel sorry for yourself until the alarm sounds. When the 15 minutes are up, ask yourself, "Is there anything I can do about this situation?" If the answer is yes, then do it. If the answer is no, say the "f" word, and get on with your life. This is peculiar because until he offered this advice, I had never heard him say a cuss word. I wish I could lay claim to that for myself. He once told me that my first words were not dada or mama, they were 'Oh tit,' when I hit my head trying to walk under the kitchen table. I had trouble with the 'sh' sound.

He's been gone now for over 30 years but I can still hear his voice and remember him fondly. I can even revisit some of his less sterling qualities and still smile. I'm glad I knew him and that I was in his sphere of influence for 35 years.

A fatherless woman's tale of love and grace

By Dorothy Rowley, bonus daughter of Eddie Radden Jr.

I never knew my biological father.

Seems he abandoned me when I was about six months old. He and my 18-year-old mother were never married because he was already married with two young children. My mother never knew this until after I was born.

But he did pay child support – for about three months. And, that was only after my mother's parents had him hauled into court where my father freely admitted paternity. They say he even held me in his arms that day for the first and last times.

Because my mother and I still lived with her parents, he was ordered to pay my grandparents five dollars a week for my care.

Like I said, that lasted a few months, as my father's marriage busted up and he fled to New York City. I learned years later, that he was murdered while gambling.

Anyway, shortly after my first birthday, my mother met and married my stepfather.

At first, he thought I was absolutely the cutest and most adorable little chocolate baby girl he'd ever laid his eyes on.

Then, as time went on and I got older, the truth came out and he began to say things to remind me and my mother that I was not his "real" daughter.

For example, because of my dark complexion, he'd call me "Darky" just so his nieces and nephews would have a great laugh – all at my expense. How that hurt, but I pretended it was Ok, and laughed with them.

I think I was about eight years old when he told me that I was the cause of his marriage with my mother not working. Another time, he shouted out to my mother that I was a jinx on their marriage. When I was about 11 years old, he told me that I had a big behind. Despite that fact that I was academically inclined, he'd shout out (I guess in a jealous fit) that I was just pretending to be smarter than my four half-siblings. Many times, if he wasn't coming up with a way to get people to poke fun at me, he'd find a reason to ridicule how quickly I caught on at school or whatever. Now that I look back, seems as if as a little girl, I'd become a sounding board of sorts for masking his own inadequacies.

When I turned 15, he bought my first pair of stockings and heels, and I was totally elated. While I thought it was odd that a father would buy a daughter such a gift, I finally felt that he really loved me.

But it wasn't too long after that he was up to ridiculing me again. Nothing extremely harsh, but still enough to still make me feel hurt and increasingly inferior.

He blurted out to my mother that, "She's gonna have a baby before she finishes high school!"

Now, mind you that since I'd never had the slightest inclination of being sexually active until long after high school, as I think back on his statement, I believe it was a precursor for what he probably had in mind for me.

And, lo and behold -- one night when I was 16 years old, and while my mother was away at her overnight job -- he tried to force himself on me.

As he awakened me from my deep slumber, the first thing I noticed was what appeared to be a large blade that he held close to my throat, like he was using it to silence me as my siblings slept nearby.

Quickly realizing what was about to happen, I immediately went into self-protect mode, begging and pleading for him to "PLEASE" leave me alone. I remember he kept telling me in a hushed tone to keep quiet. I also realized that his breath smelled nasty – like old, sour liquor.

Then he said it was something he'd always wanted to do, which made me struggle even harder!

Kicking into full self-protect mode, I must have put up a gallant fight, because he immediately gave up in frustration and disappeared into the stark darkness.

I was traumatized; yet managed to fall back asleep. When morning came, I prepared for school as usual. I don't recall seeing him anywhere in the house, or maybe I made extra efforts not to see him at all.

I didn't tell anyone – mainly because I was afraid of not being believed.

After all, my stepfather had become quite adept at making people (particularly his side of the family) think that because I was not his real daughter, that I had "issues."

But after that, life around him was never the same.

I feared and, at times, despised him. While I reasoned that he must have had some kind of illness to subject me to such horror, I still avoided being alone with him.

To his credit, he never attempted to accost me like that, ever again. I think maybe after coming to his senses, that he was truly embarrassed by his actions and just didn't know how to say he was sorry.

So, I never breathed a word of what happened that night to my mother until several years after his death. She was mortified and asked me to forgive her for not being there to protect me.

All those years went by – along with the hurt, shame, pain of feeling like an outsider -- and my stepfather had never really embraced me as a daughter.

Well, not until the day after I graduated from high school: I'd been 18 years old for the past eight months, and he said to me with the widest smile on his face, that he was proud of me and wanted to adopt me . . .

I felt totally offended! Humiliated! Of course, the adoption never happened . . .

Fast forward to now, and the only man -- other than my maternal uncles and grandfather— all of whom in their own way, gave me some semblance of fatherhood – I have even come to revere as a father-like figure is Eddie L. Radden Jr., whom I have always affectionately called, "Mr. Radden."

I first met him when I was nine years old. It was at church. . . the same church that more than five decades later, generations of my family and his still attend.

Here he was, Mr. Radden, with that warm and infectious smile. I was just a child, but everything about him told me that he loved children!

He was married and had five children (another would be on the way in a few years) of his own. Yet he found the time be so kind, considerate, and nurturing to children, who like me, longed for a father like him.

I always saw myself as a creative child who loved the arts – particularly when it came to song, dance, writing and acting.

I'd developed my interest in acting from reading my school books and imagining I was one of the characters.

Then one of my elementary school teachers chose me for a role in a play where I sang and danced. I was so proud of myself but felt let down when neither my mom nor stepfather was in the audience to cheer me on during the performance. My mom was hard at work to feed us and keep a roof over our heads. My stepfather probably just wasn't interested.

Then one day during a school assembly, I saw this little girl recite Paul Laurence Dunbar's poem, "In de Morning." I was blown away! I knew I could recite it just as well and started learning the poem so I could present it for a Black History program at church.

Well, when time came, I gathered my courage and recited the poem -- perfectly. At age 10, I had all the expression and intonation. I was a sassy little thing whose performance blew the whole church audience away.

However, I'll never forget that amid all the accolades I received, that it was Mr. Radden who couldn't get over my performance. He was completely mesmerized, stood up and gave me a standing ovation!

He praised and inspired me like I'd NEVER ever been praised and inspired before. I think he saw a dimmed light in me and was determined to not let it burn out.

So, it was Mr. Radden who began to give me encouragement and confidence to excel at all my endeavors. He kept at me to express my creative ability every chance I got. He taught me to not be afraid to project my soprano voice, to walk with purpose and to put my trust in the Lord.

In that warm and fatherly way of his, every chance he got, he just kept uplifting me, reinforcing that nothing is as bad as it seems, and that I had the ability to soar as high in life as I wanted. I always listened to him and endeavored to not ever disappoint him.

At that time, I must have been about 12 or 13 years old, which was also about when I began to see him in a different light -- as a man who was deeply committed to his beautiful wife and their family.

Growing up with the misconception that men didn't have much interest in or interaction with their children, in my young, adoring eyes, Mr. Radden soon became the father figure I longed for.

As far as I knew and had seen, raising children was a task that fell largely on their mothers. My understanding was that while men helped make children and were called, "daddy," they rarely played any significant role in their lives . . .

But Mr. Radden showed me that men were loving, kind, caring, nurturing and protective of their children. He showed me that men would readily go the extra mile to provide for their children and that yes, men told their children that they loved them.

As a child, longing for paternal love and affection, I never saw those kinds of fatherly displays in my house . . Over the years, Mr. Radden has continued to play a vital role in my life.

He was among the first people to cheer me on when I began my career in journalism.

He'd read my articles, cut them out of newspapers for safekeeping, and boast to anyone willing to listen about how he's known me since I was a little girl and that he always knew I had it in me to do well.

Like I said, he's always been there to cheer me on, from elementary school right through my college graduation.

He'd encourage me to speak my mind, to embrace my assertiveness, nourish my self-esteem, and to express my creativity at every turn.

This takes me back to those fun times when he and I would team up -- just as if we were father and daughter -- and perform skits – especially the Paul Laurence Dunbar poem – during Black history programs. We were a hilarious pair and our packed audiences always loved us!

Mr. Radden, now 90 years old, has been a part of my life for so long that I can't help but celebrate him as the father I never had.

When I became a proud member of Zeta Phi Beta Sorority, guess who was also there to help cheer me on? Why of course, Mr. Radden! I could hardly contain my tears when he stood up at a luncheon, full of emotion, and proudly proclaimed me as his "adopted daughter."

That time, I had no problem with the term "adopted daughter," as I truly felt part of him.

As he exalted me and expressed his unconditional love for me, I could see the admiration on the faces of my sorority sisters – and that made me feel very special – something of a "daddy's little princess," I might say.

Not every girl gets to be blessed with the love of a father – one who cherishes and readily protects her, shows her how a man is supposed treat a woman and who epitomizes the real meaning of fatherhood.

No, I didn't have the ideal father in my life as a little girl growing up and discovering the world around her. But God saw fit to quell my "father hunger" by placing Mr. Radden in my life to help navigate the path He laid out for me.

In the process, Mr. Radden became a mainstay in my life at a time when my confidence in my abilities and value as a human being could have been easily diminished or completely eroded.

He helped me to understand and deal with misplaced feelings of shame that had been at the center of a fatherless daughter's life. For me, Mr. Radden had become that paternal archetype—the loving, protecting, and advising father all girls need and/or long for all their life.

Because of Mr. Radden, I have been blessed beyond measure. I will forever be grateful for his guidance, his kind words of encouragement, his constant presence – and, yes, for the way he still dotes over me.

Can't imagine life without him

By Dr. Toni Boulware Stackhouse, daughter of Oscar Lee Boulware

My dad is by far the best father in the entire world and I mean that from the bottom of my heart. He is the most unselfish, giving person that I know. Let me start off by saying that my sisters and I have been blessed to have our dad in a world where fathers are less valued, while some fail to understand their own value in the lives of their children. I cannot imagine life without him and am grateful to God for graciousness towards me in the form of my dad.

As far back as I can remember my dad has been loving and caring for us in many different ways as a father should. He has certainly given us the best of himself and we are the better because of his presence in our life. I remember family time always consisted of us playing games with my dad like "hide and go seek." Now this game was interesting because my siblings and I would go hiding and my dad would come looking for us, but every now and then there would be a lapse in his coming to get us. Then he would come running for us during the commercial times of his television shows, and the lapse of time, yup you guessed it, his show had come back on. We also liked throwing pillows at my dad and he would come and chase us and we would go running, screaming with laughter. We always played this game when it was time to go to bed because it postponed our having to go to bed. He gave us laughter and joy; he was and still is very playful with us. So now that has translated to the grandchildren; however, it is enjoyable to watch him play some of the same games with them that he played with us.

My dad would always take us on adventures that exposed us to experiences in life that would make us strive for greater later on in life. He was planting seeds in us that would yield greatness. Surely we did not understand what he was doing back then, but as we look back, it all makes sense now. He was giving us life lessons from which we could draw in the future. They certainly helped to shape who we are becoming in the earth. Fathers give children affirmation that makes them feel like they can do anything in life and my dad certainly fulfilled this in my life.

I can remember him telling us when I was a little girl that we had to attend college; it was not optional because he knew education is one way to accessing a life that is both meaningful and fulfilling. He instilled in us that education could open doors to many opportunities to ensure that one would not be limited in life. So growing up, education was important, consequently we were expected to do well in school; that was a priority. Naturally he made many sacrifices to ensure that we attended good schools including catholic schools in many instances. He gave us the message loud and clear and it remained with us all, no matter what challenges we have had to face in life, they were all overcome to obtain our education.

We grew up in Baltimore city prior to its becoming the way it is now. My dad would take us places like downtown to the inner harbor, which we enjoyed although he would basically trick us into walking. We did not live too far from the inner harbor so we would start off waiting on the bus stop. As we waited, my dad would say, "Let's walk until we see the bus coming." Before we knew it we were at the inner harbor and excited about it. After a few times of doing this we knew we were going for a walk. While downtown we always had a ritual of going to the Woolworth's, a downtown landmark. My dad would give the four of us a dollar, which was a lot to us back then and we would spend it on a toy and or candy. That excited us every time; so much so, that we looked forward to this outing. We also would get peanuts to feed the birds. We would try giving the birds the peanuts and when they came close to us we would scream and come running and in daddy-like fashion he would save us from the birds. I can still remember the laughter between us and he seemed to enjoy us just as much as we enjoyed him. I also remember that my dad used to smoke pipes when I was a little girl and I loved when he would take us to the store to get the tobacco; it smelled so good. Oh my goodness, I still love that smell to this day. It reminds me of my dad although he does not smoke pipes any longer.

As we grew older and my dad obtained transportation, our trips became more elaborate. He would take us to the different museums and zoos, local and in other places like Washington D.C. and Philadelphia. He would pack lunches and we would be gone for the day. I remember that being so much fun. He always had something planned for us to do and it would always include him giving us the history about the place, which made it more interesting, as if he was our own personal tour guide. He seemed to know a lot about the places, as if he had researched them or just knew like dads do; they just know stuff.

Another outing with my dad consisted of looking at custom built homes. He would always take us into more affluent neighborhoods to look at the model homes. This was one of my favorites and his as well. I believe this exposed us to more options in life than we could actually afford at that moment but I believe that my dad was being intentional about this and it has definitely manifested in our lives today.

My dad was also the cook in the house he would often times make us weird but fun foods to eat like scrambled eggs with tomatoes and fried bologna. My dad loved Vienna sausages although I passed on them; not a fan at all. He would make spaghetti with hot dogs in it, another favorite. My dad loved preparing meals for and with us as we got a little older to assist. Our favorite snacks with my dad were Little Debbie's oatmeal cream pies and the peanut bars.

I remember on Saturday mornings we would have to do our chores, which included cleaning the entire house and my dad would play his favorite music by Kenny Rodgers and the house would have the aroma of cleaning supplies. We would clean together, wash clothes and end that with an afternoon outing, again all planned by dad.

Our home was Jesus Christ centered and this meant we attended church several times during the week including Sunday morning worship. Literally several times a week, Bible study, choir rehearsal and Boy Scouts. At home we had a ritual of having prayer time every evening before going to bed. During this time we had to recite a new bible verse that we learned that week and my dad would always say "Jesus wept," which would make us erupt with laughter because everyone knows this is the shortest verse in the bible. After that it was impossible for anyone to keep a straight face for us to continue with the Bible verses, so that usually ended that for the evening. He loves to be silly with us and make us laugh even now.

My dad was the disciplinarian when we were younger but as we got older I was able to see that my dad was a big ole teddy bear. So I appealed to his softer side, gave him those sad eyes and make him feel bad for scolding me for something I had no business doing. My siblings would tease me about getting over because of that. I remember one time my siblings and I got into some trouble for something we had done collectively and my dad gave out beatings to us one by one, but when it was my turn I just burst into tears and hugged him and said, "Daddy I love you." Well that ended the beatings; however my siblings never let me live that one down. I was like "Whoo I got out of that."

Talking about discipline, as I got older into my teenage years I began to view my dad as strict in how he was rearing us. He never allowed us to go to other people's houses, which I did not like at all. He would always say "I don't know them or what's going on in their house." I would think to myself, "Well it's not really your business what's going on in their house." In his effort to compromise, he would allow our friends to come over to our house but I'd much rather visit my friends' houses; however that was not open for discussion. I felt like I was missing out on some fun; it seemed harsh to me at the time, so I began to resent the fact that he was there, since most of my friends' fathers did not live in the house. It appeared to me that he was blocking me from having fun, so we clashed. But he was still dad, doing what he does and that was a lot. As we got older in high school, he became our personal driver for us and all of our friends, everywhere we wanted and needed to go. He rarely complained, if ever. Somehow I think that was his way of ensuring we were safe during our travels. The only times we did not want a ride was when we were trying to go somewhere he had already forbidden us to go, or we knew he would surely forbid us going. Some kind of way we always got busted, like both my parents had some type of radar or something.

As I got older into the dating age, my dad made it clear that we needed to have his approval before dating and it seemed very embarrassing as a young girl, although now my view is that fathers are protectors and that's just what they do. Of course my choice of a boyfriend was not my dad's choice and not necessarily because of who he was, but because my dad had much rather I focus on school and other things in life instead of getting so attached at such a young age. Well as us young people often do, I did not listen and engaged in a relationship without his permission. This caused a major rift between my dad and me, but of course I thought I knew what was best for me. That relationship led to my becoming a teenage mom and that literally broke my dad's heart. I remember seeing in his eyes all his hopes and dreams for me shattered, a look with such disappointment that I have only seen changed since I have been an adult and accomplished many things. At least that is how I have felt. This portion of my relationship with my father has often reminded me of my relationship with my Heavenly Father and how He must feel when we drift off the path He has chosen for us. This helped me to seek God for His plan for my life and get me back on track which also helped to restore my relationship with my dad. Now my dad never turned his back on me in this situation and was always there to help pick up the pieces from a broken relationship leaving me as a single mother. He never once said I told you so. He just picked up the pieces and filled in the gap with diapers and milk, gas and rent money or whatever was needed, whenever it was needed. I am so sure this was not the life he had dreamed for me; after all he spent so much time planting seeds and investing into me, clearly that was not supposed to be the plan. But as fathers do, he kept moving and he continues to fill in the gap today.

As a young adult I remember working jobs where I hardly had enough to pay bills and afford gas, groceries and lunch money. My dad would supplement what I needed. I needed gas on the regular and I would do grocery shopping at my parent's house weekly. I think my dad would tell me on purpose that they had just been to Sam's club because he knew I was coming over to get my groceries. When my co-workers and I didn't have money to eat lunch I would call my dad and not only ask for lunch money for myself, but for my co-workers as well. It became a running joke wherever I worked that I could call my dad and get lunch money for everyone.

I was proud that I had a dad that loved me so much and would do anything for me not just in words but in practice. However I was not proud that I needed so much, especially as I was getting older; it was time to grow up and take care of my own responsibilities. So I started calling less and trying to make do with what I had. Even though he would get upset if he found out I needed something and did not call. One day he told me he did not care what it was I needed that I could call for anything. This also helped me mature in my relationship with God. I know that my dad is only a measure of who God is because He created him, but there are so many similarities. God wants us to call on Him for any and everything even when we mess up and He will not judge us. He will help us put things in the proper order. I feel like God blessed me especially with my dad who will do anything for anyone. Many of our friends have adopted him as dad. He has a heart of gold and he will not allow anyone to do anything to us.

I already spoke about us being raised in a Christ centered home and many attribute that to my mother and I would agree, but you can't sleep on my dad. It has been many instances in life where my dad, who we have considered less spiritual, has been there with a word of wisdom to our surprise. Even in times when he has just called at the right moment to say, "Baby are you okay?" That brings tears to my eyes right now, because in different times in my life when things have been challenging, he would call at just the right time and I would just burst into tears. Like, Man, how did you know that I am not ok at this very moment. This leads me to believe he is in tune with our Heavenly Father. I have been blessed with a father that has definitely been there in more ways than one. I can't imagine having an absent father and I feel it is not fair for people to not have a father that is present. I certainly can see how some struggle to embrace the love of God because of the pain caused by the absence of a father. Wow what a loss for both father and child. What I do know is that my dad is one of the greatest gifts God has given to me even though I have not always valued him as such. But the older I have gotten, the more I have come to understand the impact of having such a wonderful father in my life. My dad has made many sacrifices for my siblings and me; he was not a perfect dad but he was perfect for us and for that we all are grateful to God.

Even in my adult life I am often reminded that I am a daddy's girl and my sisters and I tease each other about which of us is the favorite daughter. I think he really favors the one he is with for the moment, although we all are taking notes to make sure we get more than a fair share.

I got married late in life but it has always been clear that my dad would have to like the man I would marry. The dating process was so awkward because although I was 42, once I decided I was seriously interested in my husband I knew he had to make it through my dad and believe me this is no easy task. Well we had a family event and I brought Sam to meet the family and almost everyone was excited to meet him, of course they had heard about him. However my dad was a hard sell. I'm not sure if it was because I am the oldest and had been single for so long, or what, but he literally ignored Sam's attempt to introduce himself, which I was not aware of until later. He was having none of this. Here I was living in my own house, paying my own bills, but what my dad thought of this guy was very important to me. This first attempt did not go well at all. Can you say epic failure? This situation was causing me all kinds of anxiety, to the point of tears. At any rate we have to continue down this path because I am already smitten and Sam certainly was and we absolutely could not move forward until my dad was all in. After several attempts, including my having a formal lunch meeting with dad which was customary, he said he was in favor. But it wouldn't be over until Sam met with him to ask permission to marry me. Yes, some people still honor this tradition. When I told Sam he had to do it, although he had never done this before, he was not opposed; especially since I informed him we could not get married under any other circumstances. As I went through this process I remember some of my friends saying this was a bit much since people don't do this anymore. My response was simply, "Well we do and that is how it has to be done."

A world that values fathers less than it should, would certainly have a hard time understanding why this process was and still is, for some people, a great way to increase the likelihood of a relationship starting off in the right direction. Fathers are supposed to protect their children and someone with ulterior motives would think twice before bringing their shenanigans to someone's father. Anyway we made it through that process and Sam and I have been married for almost 4 years now and life has presented some challenges and guess who is right there by our side ensuring that we know we are not alone. Yes, you guessed it; my dad, as he has done since the day that I was born. He's been there in ways unimaginable, with all his ways that sometimes get on your nerves, like the 50 million questions my dad can ask. Sometimes when he asks, I am like,"Are you writing a book?" Although sometimes irky, he is someone I would not trade for anything in the world. My dad is a constant reminder of God's goodness in my life and I do not ever wish to think of life without having him in my life.

My dad the doc…

By Jannette J. Witmeyer, daughter of Dr. Jether M. Jones Jr.

My dad, Jether M. Jones Jr., was a doctor who made house calls and a loyal son to his East Baltimore community. Even after our family moved to West Baltimore, his office stayed put, on the east side of town. Those same little old ladies who claimed bragging rights when he graduated from Dunbar High School, Lincoln University and Meharry Medical College and saw him off to the army and back; got to claim bragging rights with him as their personal physician. He treated them in his office, at clinics, in their homes and in ours; and he wouldn't have had it any other way.

He loved his patients and they loved him. He enjoyed a hug and a smile as much as hearing a healthy heartbeat. It always seemed only natural to me that he was a doctor because he loved people so much. He loved making people feel good -- happy, not just healthy. And he also put a lot into making people feel special, which I saw in him as a doctor and a dad.

Born in 1923 in Estill, South Carolina, he was the first of three children born to Eloise and Jether M. Jones Sr., a seamstress and a tailor. My Uncle Ralph was born two years later, and my Aunt Maryann, two years after that. When my grandparents decided it was time to leave the south, they chose Baltimore City as the destination of the family's northern migration, and settled in East Baltimore's African-American community, near Johns

Hopkins Hospital. At some point, the family moved to the 2400 block of Guilford Avenue, the home where my happiest memories of my father resided.

My parents, who had been high school sweethearts, married while my dad was a student at Lincoln. I was born while he pursued his medical degree at Meharry. My mom and I lived with her godparents, who raised her pretty much from birth, until he completed med school. Then, we (including my brother, who was born in 1950) went to live with my paternal grandparents, when he graduated in 1952.

For me, the best part of living in my paternal grandparents' home was having the front bedroom. It was by far the most spacious one in the house. Even with beds set up to accommodate three occupants, there was still lots of room for whirling and twirling around in the middle of the floor. But the best part of the room was its large, three-sided bay window, with window seats that allowed me to sit and scan the entire block. Every day, I would plop onto the hard, wooden window seat, lean over and peer as far down Guilford Avenue as I could see, anxiously watching and awaiting his appearance on the block, after walking from the train station and his daily roundtrip trek to Washington, D.C. to complete his internship and residency. Even after a long day's journey, he almost always had something for me hidden in one of his coat or jacket pockets.

I will never forget my fifth birthday.

Turning five was a big deal, and I was super excited waiting for him to get home because we were having cake and ice cream after dinner. It was snowing pretty hard outside and he was late. Instead of sitting at my regular window perch, I sat in the living room, teetering on the edge of the sofa, awaiting his arrival. When he walked through the vestibule and into the hallway, his collar was up and his hair and big tweed overcoat were covered with snow. When I jumped up, he looked over at me and smiled. Then, he reached down into his over-sized coat pocket and pulled out my birthday present, a little, curly haired, brown and white, Cocker Spaniel puppy. I named my birthday puppy Patsy.

Getting a puppy was special. Knowing that my dad had brought a puppy home to me through a snowstorm made it spectacular. Seeing the happiness in his eyes, reflecting my joy, made it even better. He had a knack for making everything special.

As a newly minted M.D., my dad was invited to join the practice of Dr. Ralph J. Young, a highly-respected physician and civic leader throughout East Baltimore. Their office, located at 1532 E. Monument Street, was conveniently nestled in the heart of the community he loved; midway between the health department's Caroline Street Clinic and Johns Hopkins Hospital; north of Church Home Hospital, Chick Webb Pool, and Paul Lawrence Dunbar High School; and (most importantly) right up the street from the Arundel Ice Cream parlor. His office hours on Saturdays were kept short so he could round out the rest of the day with checking in on homebound patients and making a few other stops along the way.

Spending some of those Saturdays with him gave me a firsthand look at my dad's style of dispensing care to his patients, especially the elderly ones, for whom he only wrote prescriptions when he had no free samples to give. As we travelled throughout the community, it seemed like everyone knew him, and I got to see how much his care was appreciated. While many of his Saturday stops were wellness checks, they all seemed more like visits with family than anything else; with lots of laughter, talk about neighborhood doings and updates on folks back home.

Many times, he left his patients' homes laden with all kinds of goodies. What he came home with really depended on the time of year a visitor or parcel had arrived from the south. During the summer, they sent him home with lima beans, snap peas and watermelons. Months leading up to Thanksgiving and Christmas yielded collard greens, sweet potatoes, corn liquor, walnuts, pecans and oranges, accompanied by an assortment of homemade baked delights. There were even a couple of geese and ducks. One of his patients, Mrs. Hailstock (a regal woman, who I believe was a retired educator) always made an eggnog pie for the family for the holidays. When she found out that I was especially fond of the pie, she began making one for my birthday, just for me.

Luckily for me, house calls and Eastside visits weren't the only adventures that unfolded on his watch. After enduring years of early-morning and late-night train rides to Washington, DC, it might seem that taking a train ride would be one of the last things he'd want to do. Not my dad… Long before I ever heard the expression "Daddy/Daughter Dates," he took me on day trips to DC, where we visited the zoo, monuments and museums. Locally, we did dress-up dinners at Wilson's Restaurant, formerly located at North and Pennsylvania Avenues, and the long-gone Garrison Lounge, in Walbrook Junction.

Of course, I wasn't the only one to benefit from his gift for sharing a good time. I still remember peering from the back window of his two-toned, deep tan and cream-colored DeSoto (me on one side, my brother on the other, and my mom and dad up front), watching the lush foliage and blue skies of Virginia go passing by on long Sunday drives to Skyline Drive and Luray Caverns, where I discovered my fear of heights and dislike for being in caves. Whenever we made the obligatory trek to North Carolina for our "going down the country" family summer experience with my paternal grandmother's family, he always stopped at this little wooden stand by the road that sold perfect Smithfield ham sandwiches. I can almost still taste the soft, warm roll, wrapped around the nearly paper-thin slice of ham that burst into so much deliciousness with each bite, and the cold orange soda, to wash it down.

Because he loved people, our good times extended to folks way beyond family members until they just seemed like they were. In our neighborhoods (eastside and west), when we went to the beach, several families went to the beach together. I always thought of it as a way for everybody to have fun, especially since all of the families didn't have cars. As I got older, I often wondered if the true reason we travelled that way was because there was safety in numbers. After all, we always went to Fort Smallwood, and it was during a time that Black folks were still expected to go to Carr's and Sparrow Beaches, where our presence was welcome. But, he preferred Fort Smallwood, where there was something for everybody.

The Harrises brought their fishing rods and fished off the pier. Then, they taught all of the kids willing to pick up a worm how to hook one and reel in a catch. The water in the area roped off for wading and swimming was clean, and the sandy beach was debris-free and ripe with shells for collecting. In spite of having only one arm, Mr. Truitt always manned the grill, which was set up in an area with grass growing sparsely through a bed of pine needles over sandy ground, with trees scattered about to provide shade for the picnic tables and our beach chairs. When my mom and the others on food duty finished setting out the spread, the menu was extensive – hot dogs, hamburgers, fried and barbecued chicken, corn on the cob, potato salad, cole slaw, lettuce and sliced tomatoes, baked beans cooked in the can on the grill, assorted fruits and desserts and grilled fish, fresh from the surrounding waters.

My grandparents used to say they never knew who my dad would bring home when he came home on break from college and med school, and that practice never stopped. Just as he'd shown up with homesick international students back then, he brought colleagues from out of town or with no family in the area home for dinner and holiday celebrations. Sometimes, he even brought home random strangers with whom he'd had some kind of encounter.

One time, he had a flat tire in the Hampden/Remington area, a community not known at that time for having a welcoming attitude toward Black folks. He didn't have any cash on him and insisted that the man who changed the tire come to our house so he could give him a few dollars. Not only did he come to our house that evening, but he stopped by on a lot of weekends afterwards and brought along his daughter, who was my age. While we hung out in my room, he and my dad would eat, drink and talk trash. The best part was seeing the admiration in this man's eyes for my dad. As he told it: when he saw my dad dressed in a suit, he didn't think changing a tire was the kind of work that he should be doing. I don't know how many Black friends this man had, but he most certainly considered my father to be his friend and was right there, front and center, at my dad's funeral.

For Christmas, my dad really worked his magic. We always bought our tree on Christmas Eve from one of the makeshift, pop-up lots run by a couple of older men, accompanied by young boys, probably grandsons, to do their hauling. Standing around a blazing trashcan, trying to keep warm, they pointed out the different kinds of trees along with the prices. We always chose what seemed to be the tallest tree on the lot, which meant the tree trunk required lots of chopping before it would fit into the tree stand. I always gathered the excess trimmings for making wreaths and other decorations. Once the haggling was done, if we were at a nearby lot, dad would slip the guys some extra dollars, and the tree would be there waiting for us once we got home.

Once the tree purchase and delivery were out of the way, we'd jump into the car and head east to make the rounds, visiting friends, relatives, patients, businesses… you name it. We always stopped to eat. Sometimes, we would have oysters and clams on the half-shell at the shucker's cart at the corner of Broadway and Monument Street. Other times, he'd pick up overstuffed, hot corned beef sandwiches, kosher pickles, and smoked white fish from Attman's Delicatessen on Lombard Street's Corn Beef Row. And, much to my mom's chagrin, on more than one occasion, he took me to a friend's neighborhood bar where I was allowed to feast on onion pickles sandwiched between potato chips, and pickled pig feet with hot sauce. But that's another story.

No matter where we went, along the way, people always seemed to find him, wanting to thank him for the special care he'd given them or a loved one; oft-times when they had no way to pay. Then, they would hug him and load some wonderful goody into the car, as a token of their appreciation. Usually, by the time we headed home, it had begun to get dark outside, but that's when the magic began.

From placing a wreath on the front door and candles in the windows to decorating the tree, we did all our Christmas decorating on Christmas Eve. While we were out and about, my mom was able to finish her cleaning without us being underfoot and had usually begun to bake cookies by the time we got home. The combined aroma of fresh-cut pine and fresh-baked cookies instantly set the mood for Christmas. While my dad went to work securing the tree in its stand, he put us to work stringing popcorn and filling Christmas stockings with nuts, hard candy and oranges. Once the tree seemed firmly in place (the first time), he handled the task of stringing the lights and garlands. Then, my brother and I began placing the bulbs, ornaments and candy canes on the bottom half of the tree. Before long, we would be exhausted, and my parents had no problem getting us to go to bed.

Keep in mind that other than delivered gifts of seasonal floral arrangements and fruit baskets, prior to Christmas Eve, there were no visible signs of the upcoming holiday at our house. So, when we went to bed, we never had a clue what we were going to get, and none of the decorations were finished. But…somehow, between office visits, clinic coverage, house calls, patients showing up at the house, and all the normal activities that accompany having a family, my mom and dad managed to buy, wrap and store presents at locations still unknown to this day. Then, they retrieved and smuggled them into the house without our knowledge in order to create the most magical Christmas wonderland possible and have it unfold before our eyes on Christmas morning, complete with a model train running through villages and stops at the base of the tree. To this day, as vividly as I recall those holiday scenes, I don't remember any of the gifts that were under the tree. It didn't matter.

On December 11, a month before my eleventh birthday, my parents gave me Jai, the baby sister that I'd been begging for, for years. She was the best Christmas present, ever!!! Even though a number of our holiday traditions changed, our Christmas Eve tree shopping and decorating habits remained intact. As the older sister, I got to be a part of making the magic happen. At least, that's how my dad made me feel, and it stuck with me.

When he passed away (just after her eighth and before my eighteenth birthday), I was determined that I would share some of the richness of my experiences with him, with her, in his absence, and I did. We had "adventures" that ranged from day trips to Georgetown for just the two of us, to overnight camping excursions with a group of friends, to at least three Jackson 5 concerts with her best friend.

Carrying on his legacy of caring for people was also important to me, and several of his patients kept in touch with our family after his passing. Through the years, on more than one occasion, I found myself providing transportation to appointments or picking up meds, just like he did back in the day. I'm certain it's exactly what he would have wanted and expected me to do.

Addendum

These are the saints who had direct and indirect influence on my spiritual journey and I list them in each of my books because their names rise up in my spirit as I remember good times and bad and the way they each touched my life. The names are in chronological order to assist my senior memory. I hope this will encourage you to write one of your own, giving thanks for the saints who have done their work, some of whom have gone on to receive their reward, while making up the great cloud of witnesses cheering us on to our own.
May God be praised for each of them and their solid contribution to my life and the many others they blessed along the way.

Magruder Scott Cockrell
William Henry Scott
Myrtle Jane Greenhill Scott
Gertie Scott Blunt
Melvin Roosevelt Scott
Hazel Martin
Rev. James Garrett
Rev. Walker H. Dawson
Susan Frances Booze Fuller
Charlotte Flowers
Geneva Johnson
Rev. Irvin Charles Lockman
Rida Bell Billups
Victoria Clark
Hattie Childs
Bessie Dawson
Mary Hodges

Barbara Jenkins Powell
Deacon Melvin Norman
Deacon George Graves
Deacon Charles Beatty
Rev. Leslie Dyson
Bettie Crest Durant
Rev. Mark A. Riddix Jr.
Mother Irene Montgomery
Doris Payton
Rev. Shirley Lowery
Deacon Harvey Johnson
Rev. Dr. Harold A. Carter Sr.
Rev. Oral Roberts
Rev. Geraldine James
Rev. Robert Williams
Rev. Dr. Barbara Whipple
Rev. Norman Whipple
Bishop Robbin Blackwell
Apostle Stanley Butler
Rev. Dr. Stacey Nickerson
Rev. Felecia Diggs
Rev. Andre Newsome
Rev. Dr. Bertha Borum
Deacon Roslyn Rodgers
Rev. Lenora Howze

Earlier Publications:

- ❖ Make yourself at home in God's love
- ❖ Mustard Seed Mondayz Too
- ❖ Tales of the Sweetheart Gang
- ❖ Have you heard of the Holy Ghost?
- ❖ Keep Walking in Prayer…until you can't come back: #StudyGuideEdition
- ❖ Mustard Seed Mondayz: weekly faithbytes for a year
- ❖ Keep Walking in Prayer…until you can't come back

Website:
WalkingWorthyNow.com
Choose "Books and other things" from the Menu to make purchases

Social Media:
Twitter: @DorothyBoulware
Facebook: WalkingWorthyNow and DorothyBoulware

Email:
allsherote@gmail.com

Made in the USA
Middletown, DE
18 March 2019